# The Quintessence of Sartrism

# The Quintessence of Sartrism

MAURICE CRANSTON

HARPER TORCHBOOKS ♦
Harper & Row, Publishers
New York, Evanston, San Francisco, London

# CONTENTS

# The Quintessence of Sartrism

# I

# Literature and Commitment

When the Nobel Prize was offered in 1964 to Jean-Paul Sartre, and he refused it, he said, among other things, that a writer ought not to let himself be turned into an institution: he should confront the world simply as a writer, not as an Academician, or a Laureate or a Prize winner. Sartre has always refused honours: just as Bernard Shaw did, and H. G. Wells and Rudyard Kipling, men who belonged to an age which thought more highly of writers than our age does; when writers had their own special pride and authority and eminence. Sartre seems almost the last of this type of immensely influential man of letters, with

1

a name which resounds round the world, and a voice which does not shrink from saying what he thinks about the political, moral, social and cultural problems of the time. More perhaps than any other man of his generation, Sartre has asserted the right of the artist to be a moralist. Or more exactly, he has claimed that the artist who is fully conscious of his place in the order of things *must* be a moralist.

The phrase that Sartre has made famous, "committed literature"—*la littérature engagée*—has come, more and more, for him to be a definition of literature as such. Literature which is not "committed" is not literature at all. And a few years ago he went so far as to say that a writer whose work does nothing to help mankind in its present predicament would do well to give up writing altogether. Sartre even suggested that if he were himself an African, he would cease to be a writer and become a schoolmaster, or do some other work to help with the practical problems of a newly liberated underdeveloped country.

I have always thought it rather significant that Sartre should be a kinsman of the great Alsatian missionary, Albert Schweitzer: for Sartre has something of the same attachment to the idea of salvation, the same intense feelings of social duty, the same con-

2

tempt for worldly values, and the same blunt, honest, almost Calvinistic rectitude. Sartre can be fairly called a puritan, because of this austerity and high moral seriousness; and also because his work has always been informed by a profound distaste for the visible world of corruption and folly.

His first work had the apt and striking title, *La Nausée* or *Nausea*. This was published in 1938, when Sartre was aged 33. It was not his first book, for he had already brought out two or three monographs on philosophy. Although he had never been promoted from the ranks of a philosophy teacher in secondary schools, or taken a doctorate, or secured a post at a university, his philosophical books earned him a certain renown. He had become one of the leading exponents in France of what was then a distinctively German school of philosophy, existentialism. Having grown up in a bilingual Alsatian family, Sartre has always spoken German well: and he has owed far more to German thinkers such as Hegel, Marx, Heidegger and Husserl than to any French school of thought. Indeed Sartre's starting point as a philosopher was his rejection of the teaching of the central philosopher of the French tradition, Descartes.

Whereas Descartes believed that the universe can

be demonstrated by reason to be an ordered system created by God, Sartre has always held that the universe is not an ordered system at all and that God does not exist. Sartre is an atheist. But he is not an easy atheist, in the manner of David Hume or Baron Holbach and the other materialist philosophers of the eighteenth century. The non-existence of God—for which Sartre uses the nineteenth-century phrase, "the death of God"—is a matter of grave concern to him. The irrational nature of the universe sickens him.

In his autobiography, *Les Mots*, or *Words*, Sartre confesses that a passion for metaphysical knowledge possessed him at a very early age. His father, a marine engineer, died of a tropical fever when Sartre was only two years old, and Sartre was brought up in the house of his grandfather, Karl or Charles Schweitzer, an Alsatian Protestant and a language teacher by profession.*

Sartre has sometimes described his own condition, as an orphan, as that of a "false bastard". He has made some of the heroes of his books real bastards, such as Edmund Kean in the play *Kean*, Goetz in the play

* See the "Bibliography" at the end of this volume.

*Le Diable et le Bon Dieu,* (known in English alter-
natively as *The Devil and the Good Lord* or *Lucifer
and the Lord*) and has developed an elaborate theory
of illegitimacy in his book on the ex-criminal writer
Jean Genet, which he calls *Saint Genet.* But one thing
is quite clear. Sartre did not lack a "father figure" in
his childhood. His grandfather enacted the paternal
role: he might even be thought to have overacted it.
For Karl Schweitzer, with his massive presence and
gleaming eye and flowing white beard looked like
nothing so much as popular nineteenth-century images
of God.

In his home Karl Schweitzer was a stern ruler.
Sartre's widowed mother was treated, he tells us, "like
an unmarried daughter who has produced an infant".
Nobody respected her. But Sartre himself enjoyed the
situation. His mother belonged to him. He had no
father or brother or sister to "dispute his peaceful
possession of her". He was spared what he calls "that
harsh apprenticeship—jealousy". He had, he says, no
early experience of hatred and violence. One may well
wonder, in this case, why hatred and violence came to
play so large a part in Sartre's writings—not only in
the novels and plays, with all those shootings and tor-
tures, but also in his theoretical books, in *L'Etre et le*

*Néant* (*Being and Nothingness*), where all human relations are said to be forms of conflict, and the *Critique de la raison dialectique* (*Critique of Dialectical Reason*), where all human groupings are said to be based on fear, violence and terror. Conceivably Sartre was so unfamiliar with violence and hatred in his childhood that when he did meet these things they had a shattering impact.

Sartre was a lonely child. But once he had learned to read, books filled his life, and provided a way of living in the imagination for a child who had no companions. And it was from books that he learned about the world. But of course, as Sartre himself points out, the world one learns about from books is an ordered world, assimilated, classified, ticketed, systematic. Learning about the world in this way was responsible, Sartre thinks, for the "idealism" it took him thirty years to get rid of. Here we can see a clear link with the theme of his first—and still perhaps, his best—novel, *La Nausée* or *Nausea*. Roquentin, the central character of *La Nausée*, yearns for a universe which is perfectly harmonious and necessary like the universe of Descartes or Leibnitz or Newton; he is quite literally sickened by the empirical, visible universe which is contingent, messy and purposeless. Only at the end of the novel does the hero find a way of reconciling himself to reality as it is. And this has doubtless been Sartre's own problem: to cure himself of a metaphysical hunger acquired, at least partly, by learning from books instead of from experience.

Another thing Sartre tells us in his autobiography is that he did not relish being alive. He regarded his own birth as a necessary evil. Death became what he calls his *vertige;* it possessed the power of both fascination and dread precisely beause he did not like life. In his early fantasies of heroism, death was wedded to glory. He wanted death and feared it. Sartre suggests that this ambivalence lies at the root of most of our deepest intentions: projects and evasions inseparably linked. His own "mad enterprise" of writing was a way of earning a pardon for living. Writing was his salvation in the sense that it served as a form of expiation of the guilt of being alive.

Many of the things Sartre tells us about himself in his autobiography are not only expressed in language drawn from religion, but seem somehow to belong to the story of a search for grace. All he tells us about his alienation from his fellow creatures, from life and from the visible world seems like the first part of the biography of one who finds fulfilment in the contemplation of the invisible world and in the love of God. Indeed, Sartre admits that he might have found God. His grandfather, the son of a Calvinist pastor, was an anticlerical who had only an intermittent faith; his grandmother had a peacefully sceptical disposition. But Sartre's mother was a believer, who found a secret consolation in religion, and she sent Sartre to a Catholic priest for instruction. Young Sartre said his prayers. He once even had the sensation of the presence of God. Then his faith petered out. His, he says, was a "lost vocation".

The first existentialist, Kierkegaard, was a passionate Christian, and it was the purpose of his existentialism to suggest that the proof of Christian teaching could never be derived from rational arguments about the nature of Creation, but was something directly experienced in the lonely anguish of the sinner separated from God. Even in our own irreligious age there must still be millions for whom the feeling of living in a world without a Heavenly Father would be intolerable. Without God they would dwell in darkness. The hero of Sartre's first novel is in just this condition. To Antoine Roquentin, the thought of living in a universe which is not a rigid and predictable system moving according to inexorable laws is a terrifying thought. Sartre is an atheist who understands men's thirst for God, and who teaches them that they must learn to live with that thirst forever unsatisfied.

In *La Nausée* Sartre's hero passes his days, anxious and tormented by disgust and deep apprehension. In his feelings of dread Roquentin becomes conscious of the unpredictability of the universe; but in passing from his dread to the cause of it, he learns new truths. If the universe is contingent, it is also free. Because contingency is itself the only absolute, it is "the perfect free gift". "All is free", he tells himself as he sits on a park bench in a dismal French city, "this park, this city, and myself". Freedom, therefore, is not something to be found in running away from commitment; it is already there, in the universe, in his own conscious being.

This is another of Sartre's main themes: perhaps his most important. If a man is free, it follows that he is responsible for everything he does. He is not just a cog in a machine, a creature of circumstance or destiny, a puppet, or a robot. A man is what he makes himself; and for what he makes himself he alone is answerable. At the end of the novel Roquentin has another, and decisive illumination; this is perhaps his moment of conversion. He has a favourite record, the

9

American jazz song "Some of These Days"; a waitress in a café puts it on the jukebox for him. As he listens, pictures pass through his mind. He imagines a Jewish musician in a hot apartment in New York finding a reason for living by creating this simple little song. And he asks himself: "If he, why not I?" Why should I, Antoine Roquentin, not make a reason for living, give a meaning to life by doing something creative? By writing? If so, the book must be something created by Antoine Roquentin himself. So he decides to write a novel. He says to himself:

> Naturally at first it would only be a troublesome, tiring work; it wouldn't stop me from existing or feeling that I exist. But a time would come when the book would be written, when it would be behind me, and I think that a little of its clarity might fall over my own past. Then, perhaps, because of it, I could remember my life without repugnance.

Thus *La Nausée* ends. It is a marvellous book. Although the hero's problems are dramatised, everything is worked out with impeccable logic. Each stage of Roquentin's enlightenment follows rationally one from the other. All is beautifully ordered: in this, as in other ways, *La Nausée* is clearly a philosopher's novel. In places it is oddly disturbing, because we are made not only to see, but to sense what it feels like to be Roquentin going through this crisis in his life. As I have said, Roquentin finds a purpose for living in art, in writing a novel. The moral of *La Nausée* is that everyone must work out his own reason for living; but plainly Sartre himself at this stage of his life was thinking in terms of salvation through art. His attack on the uncommitted life is fully mounted in this first novel; but his concept of commitment is not yet given any specific political content. *La Nausée* is an existentialist novel; but it is nowhere recognisably the work of a socialist.

Indeed Sartre has told in his memoirs that he was "converted to politics" during the German occupation of France, largely by the influence of the Marxist philosopher Maurice Merleau-Ponty. During the 1930's Sartre regarded himself as a socialist, but he did not feel the need to take any active interest in politics. At the general election of 1935, when the Popular Front government was returned, Sartre did not even trouble to vote. In a vague way, he felt that socialism was coming, without his doing anything about it. His notion of commitment was moral rather than political.

However, it was one of the features of the general crisis of the 1930s and 1940s that the central moral problems of the time came to be increasingly inseparable from political problems; and Sartre has always been a writer with a keen sense of the immediate, of the contemporary. His second novel was a three-volume sequence, called *Les Chemins de la Liberté* or *Paths to Freedom* which traced the experience of a man of Sartre's own age living through the events of France in Sartre's lifetime. It is an attempt to show what kind of use each man makes of his freedom, either by accepting or evading the responsibility which each man equally bears for what he does.

In an essay entitled *Qu'est-ce que la littérature?* (*What Is Literature?*) published in 1948, Sartre made the point that French writers of his generation, having lived through the experiences of the War and the German Occupation, had necessarily to produce a "literature of extreme situations". Events of this time had made everyone "touch his limit". Having said this, Sartre went on to make the more controversial claim that all writers of his generation were "metaphysical writers" whether they liked the name or not.

Metaphysics, he added "is not a sterile discussion of abstract notions . . . it is living effort to embrace from within the human condition in its totality".

Sartre then named André Malraux and Antoine de Saint-Exupéry as writers of his own generation, because, although they began publishing at an earlier date, they had the same conception of what literature should be. Malraux had recognised that Europe was already at war in the early nineteen-thirties, and produced a "war literature" while the leaders of the so-called *avant-garde* of the time, the surrealists, were still producing a "peace literature". Saint-Exupéry had adumbrated a "literature of construction" to replace the traditional bourgeois "literature of consumption". These had become the guiding ideas of Sartre's own generation.

He went on to say:

*. . . we were convinced that no art could really be ours if it did not restore to the event its brutal freshness, its ambiguity, its unforseeability; if it did not restore to time its actual course, to the world its rich and threatening opacity, and to man his long patience.*

*We did not want to delight our public . . . we wanted to take it by the throat. Let every character be a trap, let the reader be caught in it, and let him be tossed from one consciousness to another as from one absolute and irremediable universe to another similarly absolute; let him be uncertain with the very uncertainty of the heroes, disturbed with their disturbance, flooded with their present, docile beneath the weight of their future; invested with their perceptions and feelings as by high insurmountable cliffs . . .*

This paragraph should perhaps be read in connexion with Sartre's remark about the German Occupation, that it brought one "to the deepest knowledge a man can have of himself. His capacity for standing up to torture and death". At the same time Sartre said he also believed that "in order to understand something about mankind, it was necessary to scrutinise extreme cases".

Sartre's theory of committed literature has led him to be highly critical of those writers who do not share his opinions. An example of this is his essay on the nineteenth-century poet Baudelaire, which he wrote at the end of the war. Sartre's reading of Baudelaire's biography is all the more interesting because of certain resemblances we may notice (but must not overemphasise) between the childhood of the poet and that of Sartre himself. Sartre attributes great significance to the fact that Baudelaire's father died when the poet was six years old (Sartre's own father having died when he was two). Between Baudelaire and his widowed mother there grew up, Sartre suggests, a bond of mutual adoration. Mme Baudelaire was at once her son's idol and his comrade. He was indeed so enveloped by her that he scarcely existed as a separate person. And precisely because he was so absorbed in a being who appeared to exist "by necessity and divine right", the young Baudelaire was protected from all uneasiness. His mother was his Absolute.

But Baudelaire's mother remarried and the boy was sent to a boarding school. This, says Sartre, was the turning point in the poet's life. We must notice that Baudelaire was only seven when his mother remarried. (Sartre was twelve when his mother took that step.) As a result of his mother's remarriage, Baudelaire, Sartre suggests "was thrown into a personal existence". His Absolute had been taken from him. The justification for his existence had gone. He was alone, and in his solitude he discovered that life had been given him "for nothing". It was at this point also, according to Sartre, that Baudelaire made his mistake. The future poet concluded that he was destined to be "for ever alone". In fact, says Sartre, we may here discern the original choice of Baudelaire. Baudelaire decided to be (as he put it) *"éternellement solitaire"*. He did not discover solitude in his destiny; because, of course, for Sartre there is no such thing as destiny to discover. Baudelaire, in his freedom, chose solitude. He wanted it, because he wanted to feel unique.

Sartre notes how Baudelaire escapes from his feeling of *vertige* into literary creation. But the trouble is, says Sartre, that the poet does not extend his creativeness to the realm of moral values. Baudelaire simply accepts the bourgeois Catholic ethics of his mother and his step-father. The result, since he does not lead the life that the bourgeoisie approves of, is that Baudelaire is possessed by an acute feeling of sin. Sartre's argument is that if Baudelaire had rejected the parental moral code, and worked out a new morality of his own, he could have been saved. Sartre has further reproaches to address to Baudelaire. The poet's fault was not only that he resisted any kind of commitment, but that he resisted any kind of socialist commitment. First Baudelaire acquiesced in the morals of the bourgeoisie, and then he also acquiesced in the reactionary politics of the Second Empire. All the poet cared about, says Sartre, was to be "different". And Sartre contrasts this attitude with that of George Sand, Victor Hugo, Marx, Proudhon, and Michelet—the progressive writers of the nineteenth century who taught that the future could be controlled, and society changed for the better.

*Baudelaire* is one of the best written of Sartre's essays but it is undoubtedly also one of the cases where his puritanism becomes extreme. In what is supposed to be a piece of literary criticism, the thought that Baudelaire was a great poet is given hardly any consideration at all. Sartre fastens instead on Baudelaire's remark without a poem being an *"objet inutile"* (a useless object), as if this were the supreme truth. One has the impression, as Professor Philip Thody has said, that Sartre "would have preferred Baudelaire to have been a third-rate early socialist pamphleteer rather than a first-rate lyrical poet". But one must not be unfair to Sartre. Even in his most enthusiastic left-wing moments he has resisted the aesthetic prejudices of ordinary Marxists.

And in one of his latest works, an essay on Flaubert which was serialized in his monthly journal *Les Temps Modernes*, Sartre has defended the great nineteenth-century novelist against conventional Marxist criticism. Sartre is as quick as any ordinary Marxist to classify and castigate Flaubert as a bourgeois. But this is only the beginning. What is more important about Flaubert, says Sartre, is not that his class was petit-bourgeois but what he did to rise above that class. Flaubert, as Sartre expresses it, "to escape from the petite bourgeoisie, threw himself across several fields of possibility towards the alienated objectification of himself and created himself ineluctably and indissolubly as the author of *Madame Bovary* and as the petit-bourgeois he refused to be".

Sartre gives Flaubert's career as an instance of the project—*le projet*. And this is an existentialist concept Sartre has often used before. It figures prominently in his principal work on ontology, *L'Etre et le Néant* (*Being and Nothingness*), where the "project" expresses the way in which a person chooses his mode of living and creates himself in action.

Flaubert's project is that of creating himself as an objective being in the form of an author, or more precisely the author of *Madame Bovary* and other specific works. Sartre writes:

*This project has a meaning. It is not simple negativity, the flight (from the petit-bourgeois predicament)—through it, the man aims at the production of himself in the world as a certain objective totality.*

*It is not the pure and simple abstract choice to write that makes the nature of Flaubert, but the choice to write in a certain fashion so as to manifest himself in the world in a certain way—in a word, it is the particular meaning that he gives (in the framework of contemporary ideology) to literature as the negation of his original condition and as the objective resolution of his contradictions.*

Sartre's argument is that "Man defines himself by his project". In other words, we each make ourselves what we are by what we do. No one has any *essence*. A man's being is the history of his achievement. The Flaubert we know is the one who wrote several remarkable books: if he had never written them then we should never have heard of Flaubert—or rather, the man we remember as Flaubert, would not have existed.

I think one cannot help sensing a certain contradiction between Sartre's attitude to Flaubert and his attitude to Baudelaire. Both those writers, after all, produced very substantial works; and Baudelaire's achievement was surely quite as much of a "project" as Flaubert's. The difference between the two cases is, quite simply, a political one. Neither Baudelaire nor Flaubert was a socialist. But Flaubert was against the *bourgeoisie,* whereas Baudelaire, as Sartre sees him, was really on the side of the middle-class Catholic reaction. And insofar as Flaubert was a kind of social realist, exposing the follies and falsehood of *bourgeois* life, it is not difficult for Sartre to envisage Flaubert as an artist who is on the side of revolution.

And the word "revolution" is a key word in Sartre's whole way of thinking. It must be interpreted, I believe, as a development of another idea that was central to the theory behind his early work: that is the idea of conversion. Conversion is the salvation of the individual by means of a radical inward change or transformation, such as that which is experienced by Antoine Roquentin in the novel *La Nausée.* Revolution is the salvation of society as a whole by means of a radical change or transformation of the system. And revolution is the most conspicuous feature of what Sartre understands as socialism.

# II
# Philosophy and Action

I have spoken of Sartre's abiding interest in the notion of salvation, and the related ideas of conversion and revolution. He claims in his memoirs to have undergone a form of conversion himself: something that happened during the German Occupation, when Sartre met the Marxist philosopher Maurice Merleau-Ponty, and thanks to his influence was, as he puts it, "cured of his idealism". But clearly this was not a simple conversion. For while Sartre abandoned his old "idealism", and became passionately interested in practical problems and in politics, he did not adopt Merleau-Ponty's Marxism. It was some years before

Sartre proclaimed himself an actual adherent of Marxism, and by that time he had worked out a reformulation of the theory which differs conspicuously from Marx's original doctrine.

No doubt it was not only the influence of Merleau-Ponty, but also the events of the war and the German Occupation, and still more of the Resistance movement, which stimulated Sartre's interest in the realm of the political. Before the war he had not been concerned with anything much besides the problems of individuals. His own life had been fairly uneventful. He did well enough at his school to pass into one of the great institutions of French learning, the *Ecole Normale Supérieure*. At the end of his student career he entered the competitive examination which opens the door of the teaching profession in France: the *agrégation;* and after failing in his first attempt he came top of the list in the second attempt. He studied existentialism in Germany. He became a philosophy teacher at several French provincial schools, published three or four philosophical books, and a very successful novel *La Nausée*. When the war broke out in 1939, he was aged 34, and called up for the army: but his bad eyesight gained him exemption from combatant duties. He served in the Maginot Line as a meteorological clerk, and was taken prisoner by the Germans in their invasion of France. After a year in a prison camp, he was repatriated on health grounds. He spent the rest of the war in occupied Paris, writing plays and essays and an occasional piece for the clandestine press. He made friends with a number of Communist and other Resistance groups and, at the end of the war, emerged as one of the leading intellectuals of the triumphant patriotic movement. He not only became a famous man himself, but he made existentialism famous.

Sartre was, of course, a man of the left, but he was not a Communist, and he has never been one. He was often very ready, and even eager, to accept the politics of the Communist Party; but he could not tolerate the philosophy of the Party. In this his attitude has never greatly changed. He started a literary review of his own *Les Temps Modernes* which was meant to be a forum for the Left—open to Communist and non-Communist writers alike. But Sartre's equivocal attitude to the Party led him into many impassioned disputes. He often criticised the Communist Party, but would spring to its defence if anyone else attacked it.

Sartre felt that what was wrong with Communism was that it rested on a wrong type of philosophy.

Marxism was out-of-date and needed modernising. And in due course he set himself to provide such a modernised Marxism. The fullest statement of this theory is to be found in his *Critique de la raison dialectique* (*Critique of Dialectical Reason*) published in 1960. This is one of Sartre's Germanic works, long, diffuse, replete with technical language and jargon. Moreover, for all its 755 closely printed pages and numerous footnotes, it is only one volume of a longer projected work. No one has as yet ventured to translate more than parts of it into English.

Sartre's approach to the subject is not, as he explains, purely academic. The first part of the book appeared originally in a Polish journal in 1957, when "destalinisation" had become the order of the day, and the theory is consciously put forward as a destalinised philosophy for bewildered Communist intellectuals, and as a basis for reunion between such intellectuals and those of the Left who remained outside the Party: that is to say, as something to fill minds left painfully empty by Moscow's repudiation of Stalin's teaching, and as a theoretical foundation for a new united front against the bourgeoisie. This public-spirited purpose in no way detracts from the philo-

sophical interest of the *Critique;* many of the best political theorists have had some such further motive;
the philosopher and the polemicist are often the same
man.

Sartre begins this book by paying the most lavish
tributes to Marxism and making the most modest
claims for existentialism. Indeed he says that whereas
Marxism is one of the main philosophies of the world,
existentialism is not even a genuine philosophy at all.
Existentialism is merely an "ideology". But Sartre
does not use the word "ideology" in Marx's sense. He
provides his own Sartrian definition both of that word
and of the word "philosophy". Philosophies, according to Sartre, are the great creative systems of thought
which dominate certain "moments" or periods of history, systems which cannot be got beyond (*dépassé*)
until history itself has moved on to another stage.
Thus, in the seventeenth century, the philosophical
"moment" was that of Descartes and Locke; at the
end of the eighteenth and the beginning of the nineteenth century, it was the "moment" of Kant and
Hegel; our own age is that of Marx. No philosophy
could go beyond Descartes and Locke in their time,
or Kant and Hegel in theirs; and no philosophy can

go beyond Marx today. We are compelled, Sartre says, to think in Marxist terms, whether we choose to admit it or not.

Not content with thus exalting Marxism, Sartre is at pains to diminish existentialism, the mere ideology. Ideologies, in this Sartrian sense, are little systems which live on the edge of the great systems of thought, and which "exploit the domain" of the genuine philosophies. Since the present century falls within the Marxist epoch, existentialism "exploits the domain of Marxism". Existentialism, then, Sartre writes, is "a parasitic system which lives on the margin of a knowledge to which it was at first opposed, but into which it seeks now to integrate itself".

This is a decidedly original perspective. There is also something audacious about the very proposal that existentialism should "integrate itself" into Marxism, for no two systems of thought could look more dissimilar. Two things, at least, would seem to offer insuperable obstacles to any fusion. First, existentialists believe in free will, libertarianism, indeterminism; and Sartre in particular has always put great emphasis on this. No theme is more marked and recurrent in all his work both literary and philosophical than that man is "condemned to be free". Marx, on the other hand, belongs to that tradition of philosophy which would banish the free will problem altogether. Freedom, for Marx is in Hegel's words "recognition of necessity". Marx holds, first, that all history is shaped and determined by the relations of production which spring from the inexorable laws of matter, and secondly, that men can master their destiny in so far as they understand those laws and consciously direct their action in accordance with them. Thus Marx does not admit any antinomy whatever between freedom and determinism. For Sartre, on the other hand, determinism is not only false, it is a form of *mauvaise foi*, or culpable self-deception, by means of which certain people evade their moral responsibility.

Next, there is the matter of individualism. Existentialists lay great stress on the isolation, the solitude, the "abandonment" of the individual; and no existentialist writer has stressed this more than Sartre from his earliest novel *La Nausée* to his latest play *Altona*. But Marx regards individualism as "a delusion of theory" and holds that man's true nature is a social one.

Sartre does not shirk these contradictions. He believes they can be resolved. He suggests that the trouble lies in the fact that Marxism—orthodox

27

Marxism—has become out-of-date, hidebound, dogmatic; it has lost its touch with humanity. This is where existentialism can help to renovate it; by "humanising" Marxism. Sartre goes on to make this curious prediction:

*From the day that Marxist research takes on a human dimension (that is to say, the existential project), as the basis of its sociological knowledge, existentialism will no longer have a reason for being—absorbed, transcended and conserved by the totalising movement of philosophy; it will cease to be one particular theory, and become the basis of all theory.*

Sartre insists that his quarrel is with the Marxists and not with Marx; indeed he gives an interpretation of Marx's essay on the Eighteenth Brumaire which suggests that Marx himself, in his most inspired moments, was an existentialist wtihout realising it. Sartre's complaint about the Marxists is that they are lazy. Sometimes they are too metaphysical and sometimes too positivistic. Their thinking is old-fashioned, and often it is not thinking at all, but blind assent to authority.

Many of Sartre's criticisms of orthodox Marxists hit the nail on the head. He shows, for example, how shallow is the judgment of those Marxist literary critics who dismiss Valéry as a "petit-bourgeois intellectual". Sartre agrees. Valéry is a petit-bourgeois intellectual, but the important point is that "not every petit-bourgeois intellectual is a Valéry". Sartre also demonstrates the absurdity of the Marxist critical habit of bundling together such diverse writers as Proust, Joyce, Bergson and Gide as "subjective"; he shows that this category of the subjective is not empirically viable; it is not drawn from experience; it is not based on the study and observation of real men.

"Lazy Marxists", Sartre says, reveal their laziness not only in their unreflective use of categories, but in their tendency to constitute the real *a priori*. Just as Communist Party politicians use these methods to prove that what has happened had to happen, so Marxist intellectuals use it to prove that everything is what it was bound to be. And this, Sartre shrewdly observes, is merely a method of 'exposition' that teaches us nothing. It cannot teach us anything because it knows in advance what it was going to find out. Hence the need for giving Marxism a new method.

Sartre describes this new method which existentialism offers Marxism as "heuristic" that is to say, it is a method serving to discover truth; it is also, he says, "dialectic". Sartre asserts that whereas the lazy

29

Marxist when confronted with any problem immediately refers to abstract principles, his own new method works by no other means than that of "cross reference" (*va-et-vient*) within the flux and movement of the real world. For example, Sartre's method would seek to explain the biography of individuals by an equally deep study of the epoch which shapes the individual and of the individual who shapes the epoch. He calls it the Progressive-Regressive method. It is progressive because it seeks part of the explanation in the aims of conscious beings; and it is regressive because it looks at the historical and social conditions in which each conscious being pursues his objectives. People have to be understood both in terms of their own aims and in the light of the circumstances which they formulate and seek to realise their aims. This has always been one of Sartre's central beliefs.

Consider the example of his play *Huis Clos* (*No Exit*) published as long ago as 1943. In this play the male protagonist Gracin tries to maintain that he has a noble and courageous nature in spite of the fact that he has done cowardly deeds, and then the *farouche* plain-speaking female character, Inès, tells Garcin that a man has no nature apart from his ac-

tions; his actions define him, so that a man whose be-
haviour is cowardly *is* a coward. The play is set in a
modern version of Hell, which lies beyond the grave.

Garcin asks Inès "Is it really possible to be a coward
when one has chosen the most dangerous way of life?
Can you judge a whole life by one act?" Inès says:
"You dream of heroic deeds, but in the moment of
danger, you run away." Garcin claims that he did not
just dream of heroism; he chose it. Inès asks for proof.
"It is deeds alone which show what a man has willed",
she tells him. Garcin replies: "I died too soon. I did
not have enough time to do my heroic deeds." "One
always dies too soon", Inès says, "or too late. And,
now your life's finished. It's time to make up the
account. You are nothing other than your life."

Garcin is an example of what Sartre calls *mauvaise
foi*, self-deception or bad faith. And Garcin, in his
bad faith, invokes the falsehood (as Sartre sees it) of
essentialism to support his pretence that, although he
has committed cowardly acts, he has a brave character
or essence or soul. It is the mission of Inès to teach him
the painful existentialist message that a man *is* what he
*does*, and no more. Garcin has no essence to be brave.
He is a coward because his deeds are cowardly. In this
connexion we must not forget one point about *Huis*

31

*Clos*—though it is one which Sartre's critics do some-times forget—and that is that all the characters are *dead*. They are no longer free beings. Their lives are terminated, and so, although they have no essences, they do have complete biographies. Put in another way, they have no future; and they can have no more freedom. Garcin is thus damned in the sense that the possibility of his ceasing to do cowardly deeds and starting to do brave deeds, and thus of turning from a coward into a brave man, is ended. Since he is dead, it is, as Inès tells him, *too late*. He can no longer be-come a brave man. Death has closed the account. Sartre's placing *Huis Clos* in Hell is therefore no mere theatrical device. It is properly placed in Hell, be-cause one of the central themes of the play is damna-tion. In this way, it explores the other side of the sub-ject of salvation, which is examined in his first novel *La Nausée*.

In his *Critique de la raison dialectique* (*Critique of Dialectical Reason*) Sartre returns to this favourite theme of his. He says again that our only nature is our history: we are what we *do*, and what we do is what we choose to do. We are totally responsible for our actions; since as beings "condemned to be free" we could, if we had chosen differently, have acted differently.

In the *Critique*, Sartre speaks of "uprooting of oneself towards existence"; and by existence, he adds, "we do not understand a stable substance, which abides in itself, but a perpetual disequilibrium, an uprooting of the whole body. And this drive towards objectification takes different forms in different individuals as each projects himself forward through a field of possibilities—of which he realises some to the exclusion of others. We call this Choice or Liberty".

I think it is clear even from this quotation alone that Sartre has retained the libertarian principle of existentialism and by no means assimilated the Marxist theory of necessity. So in spite of all that Sartre said at the beginning about Marxism being the true philosophy and existentialism being a mere ideology, it is obvious that a crucial part of the so-called integration between the two will have to be the surrender by the Marxist, and not by the existentialist, of one fundamental belief.

Then we might consider the other subject on which existentialism and Marxism are notoriously at variance: individualism. Existentialism as it is commonly understood, and certainly as it is expounded by Sartre, entails an extreme form of individualism, whereas Marxism has no more conspicuous feature than its rejection of individualism—its belief that man must be understood in terms of the social whole or common humanity. Sartre has attempted to resolve this antithesis by putting forward in his *Critique* a theory of society which he claims to be both Marxist and existentialist. How far can he be said to have succeeded?

Once again, Sartre makes free use of the kind of technical language which is favoured by Marxists. First, he invokes the notion of alienation. But Sartre, as we shall see, has a different theory of alienation from that of Marx. Whereas Marx saw alienation as the result of the exploitation of one man by another. Sartre sees alienation as an unalterable feature of the human predicament. Indeed Sartre's notion of alienation cannot be understood in purely Marxist terms. The words Sartre shares with Marx are words they have both borrowed from Hegel. Sartre's theory of alienation is an existentialised Hegelian concept, not an existentialised Marxist one. His alienation, already explained in *L'Etre et le Néant* (*Being and Nothingness*), is *metaphysical*. Nevetheless he does not forget

34

that his subject here is *sociology* as opposed to *ontology;* and that a fresh, and so to speak, specifically sociological reason has to be given for what he has always regarded as the fundamental characteristic of human relations—mutual antagonism.

This theory is developed in the most striking sections of the *Critique*. The principle Sartre introduces at this point is that of shortage or *scarcity*. Sartre says that all human history—at any rate, all human history hitherto—has been a history of shortage and of a bitter struggle against shortage. There is not enough in this world to go around, and there never has been. And it is this *scarcity*, according to the *Critique*, which makes human relationships intelligible. Scarcity is the key to understanding the attitude of men to one another, and to understanding the social structures men have built up during their life on earth. Scarcity, says Sartre, both unites and divides us, because each one of us knows that it is only the existence of others which prevents there being abundance for oneself.

Scarcity then is "the motor of history". Men cannot eliminate scarcity altogether. In this sense, men are powerless or impotent. The best that any man can do is to try to overcome scarcity by collaboration with others. But such collaboration is itself paradoxical, for each of the collaborators knows that it is the existence in the world of others that makes scarcity. I am a rival to you, and you are a rival to me. When I work together with others to struggle against scarcity, I am working with those whose existence makes that work necessary; and by my work I nourish my competitors and rivals. Scarcity then, not only shapes our attitude to the natural world, but shapes our attitude to our neighbours. Scarcity makes us all rivals, and yet compels us to collaborate with our rivals; for being impotent alone, we can only struggle effectively against scarcity by the division of labour and other such joint endeavours.

Nature, however, is "inert" and indifferent to human welfare. The world we inhabit is in part the world of nature and in part the world that has been made by our forebears in the course of their long struggle against scarcity. Sartre calls it the world of the *Practico-Inert*. The world is the world of *Praxis* in so far as it is a world shaped by the work and projects of its past and present inhabitants. This is the world to the extent that it is man-made. But the world is also the passive, or inert world of Nature on which man has had to work. Ironically, many of the things that men have done with the aim of making the world more bearable, with the aim of diminishing scarcity, have had the effect not of improving, but of worsening the world. Sartre gives the example of Chinese peasants cutting down wood to make fires and to build with; and doing this on so large a scale, that they effectively deforest their land, and so expose themselves to the hazards and disasters of constant floods. Men are tormented by their own inventions in the world of the *Practico-Inert*.

Thus, in a hostile universe, defined by scarcity, man becomes the enemy of man. In a typically Sartrian phrase, man becomes anti-man, *le contre-homme*. And in a paragraph which is dramatic enough to be a speech in one of his plays, Sartre writes:

*Nothing indeed—neither wild beasts nor microbes —could be more terrible for man than this intelligent, flesh-eating, cruel species, which knows how to follow and outwit the human intelligence and of which the aim is precisely the destruction of man. This species is manifestly our own, as each of us sees it, in the other, in the context of scarcity.*

The conflicts—or relationships of antagonism— between man and man are thus given an *economic* explanation in the *Critique*. We come next to a piece

37

of "dialectic". Antagonism is negative reciprocity; but that negation is itself negated in the collaboration between neighbours which is necessary to overcome scarcity. This is Sartre's "dialectical" theory of the origin of society.

He distinguishes two forms of social structure; one which he calls the *series*, the other the *group*. The two are significantly different. A series is a collection of people who are united only by external proximity. It does not exist as a whole "inside" any of its members. The example Sartre gives of a series is a bus queue or line. This is a collection or gathering of people that can be observed. You can look at it, count the number of people in it. Everyone is there for the "same" purpose; but they do not have a *common* or collective purpose. No one is interested in the others. Because of the scarcity of seats in the bus, each wishes the others were not there. Each is superfluous, each is one too many. But because everyone *knows* that he is one too many to the others, just as each of the others is one too many to him, all agree to take it in turn to get on the bus when the bus comes. They form an orderly series to avoid a fight on the platform of the bus. The forming of an orderly series like a queue is thus a negative reciprocal relationship which is the negation of antagonism; it is the negation of itself.

The people in the bus queue form a plurality of solitudes. And Sartre maintains that the whole social life of mankind is permeated by series of this kind. A city is a series of series. The bourgeoisie is a series of series, each member respecting the solitude of the others. But in human society, there is another kind of collection or gathering which Sartre recognises; and this is what he calls the group. A group is a collection of people who, unlike those in a series, *do* have a common objective or end. A football team is the example he gives. The difference between a group and series is inward. From the outside you cannot tell the difference. What makes a group is the fact that each member has committed himself to act as a member of that group. The group is held together, and therefore constituted, by commitment. Each member, as Sartre puts it, has converted his own individual *Praxis* into a common or social *Praxis*. The working class becomes a group when its members commit themselves to socialism. A group can get things done, whereas a series is impotent, since each member pursues only his own *Praxis*. And indeed it is precisely *because* the series is impotent that the group is constituted in the first place. The origin of the group, Sartre suggests, can be summed up in the discovery that "we must either live by working together, or die by fighting each other".

Scarcity again is the driving force, since it is scarcity, and scarcity alone which makes men work together for a common end. Scarcity is thus seen as the origin of the group. And in developing this thought, Sartre introduces three colourful notions: the pledge (*le serment*), violence and Terror. Sartre explains that the group comes into being when each individual gives his pledge to become a member of the group, and not to defect from, or betray, the group. A group is thus defined as a *pledged* group. But the pledge must be enforced, and the members must be assured that it will be enforced. This is where violence and Terror come in. It is fear of violence which drives men to form groups in the first place, and it is fear that must keep them in these groups. The fear which keeps men in their groups is Terror. Indeed the pledge itself, says Sartre, is an invitation for violence to be used against one's self if one breaks one's own word; and the existence of Terror is an assurance that violence will be used against any other member of the group who tries to break his pledge.

All groups, says Sartre, are in constant danger of dissolving into seriality. Everyone is conscious of the threat of dispersion in himself and in others. Hence Sartre can say that "Terror is the statutory guarantee, freely called for, that none shall fall back into seriality". Terror indeed is more than this: it is "mortal solicitude", for it is thanks to Terror that man becomes a social being, created such by himself and by others. Terror is the violence that negates violence. Indeed Sartre goes so far as to say that Terror is fraternity. For Terror is the guarantee that my neighbour will stay my brother; it binds my neighbour to me by the threat of the violence it will use against him if he dares to be "unbrotherly".

The most important example of a group which Sartre gives is the state. The state, he says, "is a group which reconstitutes itself incessantly, and modifies its composition by a partial renewal—discontinuous or continuous—of its members". Sartre argues that the group in fusion throws up leaders; later the group perpetuates itself by founding institutions. This is the basis of sovereignty. Authority is connected with Terror in the sense that the sovereign is the man who is authorised to exercise Terror. In a serial society, I obey because I have to obey. But in a state I obey myself because it is I, by my pledge, who have merged myself in the group and authorised the sovereign to command. Sartre does not, of course, fancy that every member of the state has actually given his pledge personally; he has been pledged *by proxy;* but the pledge is no less a pledge.

Now, Terror is not only fraternity; it is also liberty. For I freely merge my individual project in the common project when I pledge myself (or am pledged by proxy) to the state; and when the sovereign, fortified by Terror, commands me on behalf of the state, he is giving me back my freedom.

Such is Sartre's theory of social structures. How far can it be considered a Marxist theory? There is not much doubt that it is a thoroughly *Sartrian* theory, one which harmonises completely with the doctrine of human relationships put forward in 1943, in his chief work on existentialist philosophy *L'Etre et le Néant* or *Being and Nothingness,* and summed up by a character in his play *Huis Clos* with the remark "Hell is other people".* This theory is, briefly, the following: If I speak, I objectify myself in words. Those words, once uttered and heard by other people,

* L'enfer, c'est les autres.

become *things* in the external world. Other people can hear them, think about them, talk about them. My words are part of the furniture of *their* world.

Sartre developed this theory fairly fully in his earlier exposition of existentialism, where he argued that relations between people are inevitably subject to mutual tensions, because each individual, acting towards others as an objectifying Other, robs others of their liberty. This is what leads Sartre in *Being and Nothingness* to say that all relations between men are forms of metaphysical conflict, which tend either towards the sadistic or towards the masochistic. Togetherness, harmony, love, the *Mitsein* is impossible; all relationships between men are relationships of conflict.

In the *Critique*, Sartre gives a new reason for this conflict; but the conclusion is the same. He still maintains that each individual is at war with all the others; and though social groups are formed, these groups are held together only by the pledge and Terror; they are in constant danger of relapsing in the individualistic condition of the series. But there is one great difference. Conflict is no longer seen as part of man's necessary predicament or condition. Conflict is contingent. It is the result of scarcity. Remove scarcity and you remove the circumstances that have turned man into anti-man. And Sartre believes that a socialist revolution directed towards the conquest of scarcity could bring about just this transformation.

Bourgeois society, in Sartre's language, is a serial society—a series of series. But socialist society is a society of the group writ large. But a group, as he sees it, can never be a natural group. It can only come about as a result of a pledge: by a pledge that is enforced by Terror. Violence is thus for Sartre the basic feature of any social group. It would commonly be said that violence is a feature of a revolution or revolutionary movement. What distinguishes Sartre's position is his belief that violence is seen as a feature of any political grouping whatever. In calling for revolution, he does not think he is asking for the invasion of a peaceful society by an aggressive movement. Existing society is already permeated by violence, according to Sartre.

In a newspaper interview in 1962 Sartre said "For me the essential problem is to reject the theory according to which the Left ought not to answer violence with violence". It is interesting that he described this as the *essential* problem. The revolution Sartre believes in is one which answers the violence of bourgeois, capitalist, imperialist violence by the violence of a disciplined movement of liberation. He calls such violence "Terror": he does not shrink from that alarming name, but like Robespierre at the time of the great French Revolution, Sartre accepts it with a zeal and dedication that is almost religious.

# III

# Socialism and Revolution

Thirty years ago, when Sartre's first novel *La Nausée* was published, a review of it appeared in an Algiers newspaper by a very young French-Algerian journalist, who was afterwards to become famous, Albert Camus. It was not an uncritical review, but it marked the beginning of a friendship between the two writers, which was afterwards to be important for both of them, though it did not last. In the beginning, as his review of *La Nausée* shows, Camus accepted a part of Sartre's existentialist philosophy: he agreed that the universe was meaningless and that God did not exist. But Camus did not like what he afterwards called

Sartre's "Germanic" qualities: his puritanism, his fanaticism, and his love of metaphysical systems. Camus believed in what he called a "Mediterranean" philosophy of joy in life, of love of the physical universe and warm human sympathy. This difference of temperament was what led in time to the break between the two writers.

They first met during the war, when Sartre, an older and more established author, took an interest in Camus and helped to promote his reputation. France at the time was under German occupation; Camus was one of the leading fighters of the Resistance and editor of the clandestine newspaper, *Combat*. Sartre, who had been invalided out of the army, and could not participate in Resistance action, admired, even idolised, young Camus as a hero of the active and fully committed life. But when the war was over, both Sartre and Camus realised that their political attitudes were very different, even towards the war itself.

Camus felt that all war was evil; that the violence of the Resistance itself was evil, but that it was a necessary evil. Justice was, for Camus, the supreme good; and if justice could only be defended by force, then force was permissible; but it was never desirable; wherever possible, the way of non-violence should

47

be chosen. And so, just after the war, Camus, who had fought so heroically in the Resistance, pleaded for universal peace, for clemency towards the collaborators who had been arrested, and for the total abolition of capital punishment.

Sartre argued on altogether different grounds, that violence is an inescapable feature of political life. He looked on Camus as an idealist, a utopian out of touch with reality. Sartre, with his intense belief in free will also believed in retribution. He had not great desire to abolish capital punishment, least of all for fascists. Sartre's disagreement with Camus prompted him to return, in several of his works, to this theme of the necessity of violence.

His most effective treatment of it is to be found, I think, in his plays and especially in *Les Mains Sales*, literally *Soiled Hands*, but usually known in English as *Crime Passionnel*. In this play a young middle-class Communist, Hugo, is sent by the Party to kill one of its renegade leaders, Hoederer, who is making a pact with the Royalist and Liberal politicians in some Balkan country to resist the Germans. Hoederer is alleged to be selling out the workers to the old ruling class. Hugo, the appointed executioner, is a gentle idealist by nature, and ill-fitted by his upbringing to kill at point blank a man he knows. And though he tells himself that his scruples are only bourgeois inhibitions, Hugo cannot bring himself to do the job when the opportunity presents itself. A little later, however, Hugo sees Hoederer kissing his wife; then, in an excess of jealousy, he finds it easy to shoot him. Afterwards Hugo discovers that communications with headquarters have been restored, and that Hoederer's policy of collaboration with the Royalists and Liberals has become the Party Line. By then it is too late to undo what has been done, and a virtue has to be made of a necessity.

The irony of this story is so deadly that many people understood it, when it was first performed, as an anti-Communist play. But Sartre's intentions were not quite so simple. Indeed when he found that the play was being used as anti-Communist propaganda, he put a stop to its production. The most interesting character in the play, and the one by whom the author's sympathies are most clearly engaged, is Hoederer. Hoederer is the one who says what Sartre himself has to say. Now Hoederer says that a man can never be sure what is the right thing to do, but that a man must nevertheless act and take the responsibility for his actions. He tells Hugo that a man who does not want to take the risk of being wrong ought not to go into politics at all. When Hugo, in the purity of his Communist dogmatism, expresses disgust at Hoederer's plan for alliance with the bourgeois political parties, Hoederer says to him:

*How frightened you are of soiling your hands. All right, stay pure. Whom does it help, and why did you come to us? Purity is an ideal for a monk or a fakir. You intellectuals, you bourgeois anarchists, you use it as an excuse for doing nothing. Well, do nothing; stay put; keep your elbows to your sides; wear kid gloves. My hands are filthy. I've dipped them up to the elbows in blood and shit. So what? Do you think you can govern and keep your soul white?*

Here we are given an important insight into Sartre's own attitude to politics. Political action is depicted as being, of necessity, a struggle, and that struggle means violence and bloodshed. Hoederer does not want to be assassinated, but he doesn't object to assassination as such. Similarly, we may notice in Sartre's condemnation of the Soviet intervention in Hungary in 1956; he did not object to armed intervention in itself, but only to the kind of intervention which was injurious to socialism.

One of Sartre's most interesting essays in political drama is the scenario for a film which was never made, and which, though published in book form in both French and English, remains, I think, an undeservedly neglected work. It treats the same theme as *Les Mains Sales*, but in greater detail, and with perhaps a little more subtlety. The scenario which is called *L'Engrenage* (*In the Mesh*) depicts the career of a revolutionary leader, Jean, who comes to power at the head of the workers' party in a small Central American republic. Jean's country is on the frontier of a great capitalist nation, so that even as President, Jean cannot do what he wishes. He would like to nationalise the oil wells, as his party has promised, and as the people expect him to do, but he fears that if he does so the Great Power will intervene and crush his regime. His only hope is to wait until the energies of the neighbouring state are directed towards war elsewhere. In the meantime, Jean suppresses all democratic institutions in his own country as an emergency measure. But in the end, Jean is overthrown by his own left wing; who, when they come to power, find that they have to do exactly what he has done.

There are certain similarities between this character Jean and Dr. Castro of Cuba; and it was no surprise to see that Sartre became one of Castro's most eager foreign champions. But there are other points in *L'Engrenage* which are worth attention. There is a conflict of conscience between Jean and his pacifist friend, which is reminiscent both of the dispute between Hoederer and Hugo in *Les Mains Sales* and also of the argument in real life between Sartre and Camus. Lucien, the pacifist in *L'Engrenage* is less naive than Hugo; but his point of view is just as vigorously resisted.

Lucien says to Jean: "The first condition of being a man is to refuse all participation, direct or indirect, in an act of violence".

Jean listens to him, torn between friendly admiration for Lucien's integrity and the bitterness of his own experience.

"And what methods would you use?" he asks.

"Everything possible. Books, newspapers, theatre. . ."

"But you are a bourgeois all the same, Lucien. Your

father never beat your mother. He's never been flogged by the cops or sacked from a factory without an explanation or without notice simply because they wanted to reduce their staff. You've never suffered any violence. You can't feel it as we do".

"If you've suffered it", replies Lucien, "you've all the more reason for hating it". "Yes, but it's deep rooted in me".

One can readily imagine that *L'Engrenage* would have made a stimulating and successful film. But Sartre has always preferred to write for the stage; and he returned to some of the themes of *L'Engrenage* in one of his longest and most ambitious stage plays, *Le Diable et le Bon Dieu*, known in English as *The Devil and the Good Lord* or *Lucifer and the Lord*. It is set in Germany at the time of the Peasants' Revolt. The hero is Goetz, an illegitimate son of a nobleman, and one of several "bastard figures" who appear in Sartre's writings. Goetz is a fighting man who is inspired by the idea of setting up a peaceful Christian community or utopia. To begin with, he has some success; but the people who live in his model community are so imbued with the gospel of non-violence that they are unable to defend themselves against rapacious invaders, and the city is destroyed.

As a result of this experience, Goetz decides to abandon his utopian, religious dreams and return to his military trade. He says: "I want to be a man among men". And he explains what this means: that he must begin with crime:

*Men of today are born criminals; I must demand my share in their crimes if I desire my share of their love and their virtue. I wanted love in all its purity. Ridiculous nonsense. To love a man is to hate the same enemy that he hates. So I will embrace your hatred. I wanted to do Good. Foolishness. On this earth and at this time, Good and Evil are inseparable. I agree to become evil in order to become good.*

Goetz is offered the generalship of the peasants' army. He hesitates; then puts on the uniform, and promptly issues an order that all deserters will be hanged.

*I told you I would be a hangman and a butcher. Don't be afraid; I shan't flinch. I shall make them hate me because I know no other way of loving them. I shall give them their orders, since I have no other way of being obeyed. I shall remain alone with this empty sky above me, since I have no other way of being among men. There is a war to fight, and I will fight it.*

So *Le Diable et le Bon Dieu* ends. I believe it to be

a work of the highest interest and dramatic intensity.
In this play Sartre has given the argument for non-
violence and peaceful change, a more sympathetic
statement than he gives it in either *Les Mains Sales* or
in *L'Engrenage;* and Goetz is presented as something
rather less than a hero. The two sides are better bal-
anced; and yet there is no doubt where the sympathies
of the author lie.

Up to a point, we can see in this play a justification
for Sartre's own attitude to Communism. For a defence of political ruthlessness can easily be read as a
defence of Communist ruthlessness. But we must not
put too much stress on this. Sartre's aim has not been
to present the special problems of twentieth-century
socialism; his subject, rather, is something which belongs to the whole of history, as he sees it. One might
call his subject the politics of humanism; and the
play's unmistakable message is that the politics of humanism must renounce the ethics of non-violence
which belongs to the politics of religion and contemplation and quietism. The politics of humanism is the
politics of *this* world; and because this world is so
deeply touched with evil (the consequence, in Sartre's
view, of scarcity), the only way of mastering evil is to
be ruthless, to soil one's hands with crime.

Sartre said in February 1963: "If I were an Italian

I would join the Italian Communist Party". But this remark must not be taken to imply that what Sartre likes about the Italian Communist Party is its more liberal and democratic tendency, compared to that of the French Communist Party. What Sartre objects to in the French C.P. is not that it is too extreme, but that it is docile and conservative and subservient to Moscow; it is not revolutionary enough. Sartre is to the left of the Party. It is *he* who is the extremist. And this is what led to his famous quarrel with Albert Camus.

The two friends began to drift apart soon after the war, when the existence of labour camps in the Soviet Union was proved beyond any doubt. Camus asked Sartre to join in some form of protest against these camps, but Sartre refused on the grounds that to do so would be to lend himself to "Cold War" propaganda which the Americans were directing against Russia. Camus argued that in all this talk about propaganda and the Cold War, the simple human fact of the sufferings of the people in the Russian labour camps had become quite forgotten. Ideology, Camus felt, was destroying people's simple humanity.

This thought inspired Camus to write a book which really angered Sartre: *L'Homme Révolté* or

*The Rebel.* In this book, Camus resumed his attack on fanatical political ideologies of all kinds. He placed Rousseau, Robespierre, the Romantic movement, Marx, and fascism in the same tradition. Against this "Northern" tradition of fanatical ideology, Camus pleaded for "Classical" or "Mediterranean" moderation, or *mesure*, and said that it was the mark of a true rebel that he would not accept any dogmas or prefabricated creed whatever. Camus ended his book by recommending a liberal type of welfare-state democracy, achieved not by revolution, but by a gradual process of reform.

Sartre attacked this as being nothing better than conservation or, at best, a form of quietism which lent itself to the cause of reaction. After the book was published, Sartre declared his friendship with Camus ended. Sartre believed, as he has believed for over twenty years, that the only hope for mankind lies in revolution; and moreover, that anything which falls short of revolution, or which has the effect of delaying the revolution, is a *betrayal*.

The word "betrayal" is important here, and its significance is all the greater when we remember Sartre's theory of society, to which I have already referred. Sartre regards the group as a social unit held together in brotherhood only by the threat of Terror against anyone who betrays his pledge of allegiance to the common aim. Hence, for Sartre, political opposition, even political dissent, readily assumes the aspect of treachery, or even treason.

The purges conducted by the Stalinist regime in Russia did not astonish Sartre; they seemed to him only too intelligible. Correspondingly, in recent years Sartre has been quick to justify the purges in Cuba and China. His attachment to Russia grew increasingly cooler as the Russian leadership became more attached to the idea of peaceful co-existence. Sartre does not believe in co-existence; and what is more, he claims that the West does not practise it. He sees the hand of American aggression everywhere; not only in Vietnam, but in other parts of Asia and in South America too. He has long been passionately anti-American. One of his successful early plays, *La Putain Respectueuse,* or *The Respectful Prostitute,* is simply an attack on American racialism—an attack which is perhaps rather weakened by the intemperate spirit of the author. In an interview in November 1966 Sartre said: "Opposition to the Atlantic Pact ought to be the chief criterion of a politics of the Left". He explained this by saying:

The world is not dominated by two great powers,

but by one: the United States. And peaceful co-exis-

tence despite its positive attractions, really serves the

interests of the USA. It is thanks to co-existence, and

the Sino-Soviet dispute, which is largely a consequence

of co-existence, that the Americans can bomb Viet-

nam in all tranquillity.

The fact of the matter is that Sartre is very individualistic in the positions he adopts on political mat-
ters. He believes in Party discipline and strict controls,
but he will not allow anything outside himself to govern his own decisions. Typical of this is Sartre's refusal
to appear on French television, because of its being a
state monopoly; his refusal of the Nobel Prize, which
Communists like Quasimodo in Italy were quick to
accept; and Sartre's refusal to accept a professor's
chair at the government controlled Collège de France.
He also follows a distinctly unusual line on the subject
of freedom for writers. He refused to sign the appeal
for clemency for Pasternak's friend, Madame Ivan-
skaya, when she was jailed in the Soviet Union; but
he made a vigorous protest against the imprisonment
of the Russian writers, Sinyavsky and Daniel.

Clearly Sartre belongs to the tradition of Voltaire,
or indeed to the Protestant tradition of personal wit-

ness. When the Swedish Academy offered him the
Nobel Prize in 1964, the committee expressed their
appreciation of Sartre's devotion to the idea of freedom. Sartre in his reply pointed out that freedom to
him meant something very different from what it
meant to the Swedes. Sartre wrote:

*Freedom is a word that lends itself to numerous
interpretations. In the West is taken to mean abstract
freedom. But to me it means a more concrete freedom
—the right to have more than one pair of shoes and to
eat when hungry. There seems to me less danger in
declining the Nobel Prize than in accepting it. To
accept it would be to lend myself to what I would
describe as an 'objective salvage operation'. I read in
the Figaro Littéraire that my controversial political
past should not be held too much against me. I realise
that this article does not express the opinion of the
Swedish Academy. But it clearly indicates the interpretation that would have been put upon my ac-
ceptance of the Nobel Prize in certain right-wing cir-
cles. I regard this 'controversial political past' as still
valid, even though I am entirely ready to admit to my
comrades the past mistakes that I have made. I am not
implying that the Nobel Prize is a bourgeois prize; but*

*I know the bourgeois interpretation that would inevitably be given if I had accepted the prize.*

Sartre's reference in this paragraph to "concrete freedom" should not be taken to mean that this is the *only* sense in which he uses the word "freedom". For he has always believed equally in metaphysical freedom or what is sometimes called the freedom of the will. This everybody has, because it is part of the human condition. We are all free agents, responsible for what we do. It is this kind of freedom which makes "commitment" a logical necessity. Sartre once uttered the unforgettable paradox that Frenchmen were never more free than under the German Occupation. Here, of course, he was not talking about concrete freedom, but about metaphysical freedom. What he meant was that the German Occupation drove Frenchmen to that extreme limit where they were most acutely conscious of themselves as men with free will and moral responsibility.

Sartre's notion of concrete freedom, on the other hand, is substantially an economic one. To be free is to be free from bondage to natural necessity, free from hunger, poverty, misery, want. And this concept is closely tied to Sartre's basic sociological notion, that scarcity, or shortage, has been the decisive factor in shaping all men's social relationships, all our history hitherto.

Sartre's theory of a committed literature has hardened over the years. Fifteen years ago he was still sympathetic enough to purely literary innovation to write an enthusiastic preface to an experimental novel by Nathalie Sarraute. But five years later, when he was asked what he thought of a book by one of Madame Sarraute's fellow practitioners of the New Novel, Sartre said: "Do you think I can read Alain Robbe-Grillet in an underdeveloped country?" Sartre went on to offer the writer two alternatives, "two choices in the world of hunger we live in". The first was to give up writing altogether to join in the struggles of underdeveloped peoples by doing some kind of practical work. The second was to "prepare for the time when everyone will read by presenting problems in the most radical and intransigent manner".

It is worth remembering that Sartre's kinsman, Albert Schweitzer, once expressed sentiments very similar to these, and, choosing the first alternative, forsook the vocation of a scholar and went to work as a medical missionary in Equatorial Africa. Why does Sartre's reasoning not carry him in the same direction?

Presumably because he feels that such work would be purely philanthropic; while he, with his special gifts and influence, can be of more use writing books which, as he puts it, present problems in the most radical and intransigent manner.

It is a long time since Sartre wrote a play, and even longer since he wrote a novel. True, he has written a short autobiographical work, *Les Mots*, or *Words*, which came out in 1963, and a critical essay on *Flaubert*, which appeared in serial form in 1966. Even so, his most substantial work in recent years has been his *Critique de la raison dialectique* (*Critique of Dialectical Reason*), of which so far only the first volume has been published.

In this book Sartre comes before us as a philosopher in the classical tradition, as one who frankly assumes the duty of telling men how to live and think. Simone de Beauvoir in her memoirs tells us something of the effort it has cost Sartre to produce this vast work. She is well qualified to speak, since without actually marrying Sartre, she has been his partner in life for over forty years. Simone de Beauvoir tells us that Sartre used to sit up for most of the night, keeping himself awake with coffee and pills, for months at a time, in order to write his *Critique*.

Sartre has always taken to heart his own doctrine that every man is responsible for everything he does; and he has an acute sense of the responsibility that he himself bears as a writer whose words are listened to by a large public, and who is looked on as a kind of leader by a great many young intellectuals all over the world. He has tried to use this influence to make liberal intellectuals more socialist, and socialist intellectuals more libertarian.

# IV

# Imperialism and Liberty

Sartre has long been a bitter critic of imperialism or colonialism. And he criticizes imperialism very simply in the name of liberty. Imperialism for Sartre is nothing but domination; he condemns it and loathes it. This he has done since he first became interested in politics. His attitude is significantly different from that of Marx and the European left generally. For Marx took what he could fairly claim to be a "historical" view of imperialism, and not a moralistic one. He saw imperialism as part of the flowering of the bourgeois phase of history; and because it carried capitalism and progress into the feudal East and into sleeping Africa, it represented a decisive moment in the dialectical passage of mankind from slavery to socialism. Marx's attitude was rooted in his determinism; Sartre's is rooted in his existentialist philosophy of human freedom. Sartre is rarely able to achieve a detached historical perspective. He regards imperialism as an evil exercise in exploitation, and the only history he has to offer is an indictment of it.

If Sartre's approach to imperialism is thus at variance with that of Marx, it is still more at odds with that of the Communists. The French Communist Party has always had an ambiguous attitude to imperialism. This is partly because the USSR, which the Communists defend, has itself been an imperialist power, extending its frontiers and crushing national independence in the Baltic States and elsewhere. The French Communists have also often felt it to their advantage to uphold French imperialism, if only for the sake of keeping discipline over a wider society of French-speaking Communists, and deploying the power of a world-wide state on the side of the USSR against others. Hence the French Communists have often upheld imperialist institutions in practice while condemning "imperialism" in the abstract. Sartre, in contrast, has been squarely and unequivocally anti-imperialist. His views have perhaps been overzealous, and unworldly, and unresponsive to the realities of practical politics, but they have, at any rate, been consistent.

In the 1950's Sartre devoted a great deal of his time to pamphleteering on behalf of the movements in Indo-China and Algeria which were trying to overthrow French rule. In *L'Affaire Henri Martin* (1953) he took up the cudgels on behalf of a naval officer who had been imprisoned for distributing leaflets in support of the Indo-Chinese nationalists. Sartre attacked the official government view that French forces in Indo-China were defending the rule of law against Communist terrorists, and claimed that Ho Chi Min was leading a popular movement of liberation rather than a Communist rebellion. But Sartre did not offer much in the way of evidence or history to support this analysis. On the subject of Algeria he wrote in greater detail, as indeed he had to, since the situation in that country was more familiar to his readers. It could not so easily be represented as a confrontation between an alien power and an exploited native people, since Algeria was formally a province of the French Republic and the population consisted of a large minority of French-speaking settlers side by side

67

with the Arab majority. Many liberals, including Sartre's erstwhile friend Albert Camus, believed that a policy of reconciliation between the settlers and the Arabs in Algeria was better than yielding to the terrorist methods of the FLN and submitting the minority to the dominion of the Arab nationalists. Sartre's reply was to assert that the relationship between France and Algeria had always been one of economic exploitation, and that the settlers were mere agents of this exploitation.

In an article entitled *"Le Colonialisme est un système"*, published in *Les Temps Modernes* in 1956, Sartre argued that the introduction of French political rule in Algeria in the 1870's was used to facilitate certain economic changes—namely to enable French settlers to buy land cheaply from the Arabs, and thus to transform Algeria at once into a garden helping to feed metropolitan France and a protected market for the products of French factories. In this article, Sartre turned, in a somewhat uncharacteristic manner, to statistics. He noted that the production of cereals for Arab consumption had fallen backward in Algeria while the production of wine, which the Arabs did not drink, had multiplied enormously; that land owned by European settlers rose from 115,000 hectares in 1850 to 2,703,000 hectares in 1950, and that while nineteen million Arabs currently produced only 48 million francs worth of agricultural produce, one million settlers produced 92 million francs worth.

Sartre never paused to consider that these figures might be taken as evidence of greater industry and efficiency among the settlers, nor did he try to explore the sociological and historical factors which made the Arabs of Algeria, like the Arabs of the Middle East, economically backward and unproductive. He was content to blame imperialism. And a simple diagnosis pointed a simple solution. Remove French power and all might be well. In the event, only a simple solution was demanded. Neither the Arabs nor the settlers wanted reconciliation. The settlers called on French counter-terror to answer Arab nationalist terror, and when it came to a choice between one extreme and another, the Arab nationalists won. That victory was in a sense a victory of revolution over counter-revolution, and Sartre took the events in Algeria as confirmation of his own belief in the primacy of violence in politics.

At the time of the Algerian war, Sartre made the acquaintance of a young intellectual in the FLN who was to produce a book which has since become a classic of anti-imperialist literature: Frantz Fanon, the author of *Les Damnés de la terre* (*The Wretched of the Earth*). Sartre had an undoubted influence on Fanon, and Fanon, in his turn, had a certain influence on Sartre.

Fanon was a black psychiatrist from the French island of Martinique. He had been elaborately educated into the French culture and enabled to earn his living as a member of the French professional *élite*. But as the result of several humiliations to which he was subject as a Negro even under the supposedly egalitarian French system, Fanon came to repudiate the whole imperialist project of turning "natives" like himself into imitation Frenchmen. Working as a psychiatrist in a hospital in Algeria, he found himself more and more sympathetic towards the Arab nationalists, and he eventually quit his employment under the French government to join the FLN. Fanon had once leaned towards Communism, but he turned against the party when he came to feel that it was dominated by the interests of its European members. So Fanon attempted to work out a political theory of his own as an alternative to Communism. This was the basis of his friendship with Sartre, who was trying to do much the same thing.

Fanon seems to have sped up the process of Sartre's disenchantment, not only with the French Communist Party, but with the European working class. He seems also to have encouraged Sartre to believe that the Third World might provide the proletariat needed to effect a revolution. The workers of the industrialized West were clearly failing to enact the rôle assigned to them by Marx; far from overthrowing the *bourgeoisie*, they had, with improved standards of living, more or less joined the *bourgeoisie* themselves. The workers of North America were the most *embourgeoisé*, but the workers of Western Europe were rapidly catching up. Sartre was beginning to doubt the possibility of the French workers' attaining a revolutionary class consciousness. Hence Sartre's response to Fanon's vision of an alternative proletariat—the hungry peasants of Asia, the submerged masses of South America, the coloured races who had been exploited by imperialism everywhere, including the Negroes in the American ghettos, the wretched of the earth, the *damnés de la terre*, as Fanon called them in the title of his immensely successful book. Here, conceivably, was a class of persons poor and angry enough to become the agents of an historical transformation.

Fanon believed in the necessity not only of a new

revolutionary proletariat, but also of revolutionary violence; and Sartre, in the preface he wrote in 1962 for Fanon's *Damnés de la terre*, endorsed Fanon's views on violence with palpable enthusiasm. Sartre may even be thought in his enthusiasm to have some-what distorted Fanon's views. Fanon's main point was that it was better for a new country to have fought for its independence than to have had that independence granted peacefully and legally by the departing European powers. One of the reasons for this was Fanon's mistrust of the kind of indigenous ruling *élite* which was emerging in the Third World, and simply replacing the alien rule with a native despotism of its own. Fanon was a passionate believer in popular democracy, and he was bitterly disappointed by the kind of régime he found in the newly independent states of West Africa when he went there as an envoy of the FLN. No doubt he would have been equally disillusioned by the kind of régime which the FLN itself set up in Algeria after its victory. But Fanon did not live to see the outcome. He died in 1961, at the age of 36, before the Algerian War had ended.

In his preface to *Les Damnés de la terre*, Sartre recorded his agreement with Fanon's belief that Europe was doomed:

Europe is done for. A truth which is not pleasant to state, but of which we are all, convinced are we not, fellow-Europeans?—in the marrow of our bones.

Despairing thus of Europe, Sartre looked to the Third World: where revolution was really conceivable "in those countries where colonisation has deliberately held up development, the peasantry, when it rises, quickly stands out as the revolutionary class. For it knows naked oppression, and suffers far more from it than the workers in the towns, and in order not to die of hunger it demands no less than a complete demolishing of all existing structures".

Sartre gave his own reason for agreeing with Fanon that the colonial people's struggle for independence should be violent: imperialism itself, he wrote, is violent, and "no gentleness can efface the marks of violence: only violence itself can destroy them". He goes on to say: "The native cures himself of colonial neurosis by thrusting out the settler through force of arms. When his rage boils over, he rediscovers his lost innocence and he comes to know himself in that he himself creates his self . . . When the peasant takes a gun in his hands, the old myths grow dim and the prohibitions are one by one forgotten. The rebel's weapon is proof of his humanity. For in the first days of the revolt you must kill: to shoot down a European is to kill two birds with one stone, to destroy an oppressor and the man he oppresses at the same time: there remains a dead man and a free man; the survivor for the first time, feels a *national* soil under his foot".

With rhetoric of this sort, Sartre made Fanon's plea for violence seem rather more irrational—and even fascistic—than it seems in the book itself, especially as Sartre linked it to a plea for hatred:

> Make no mistake about it, by this mad fury, by this bitterness and spleen, by their ever-present desire to kill us, by the permanent tensing of powerful muscles which are afraid to relax, they have become men . . . Hatred, blind hatred which is as yet an abstraction, is their only wealth.

Readers of Sartre's novels and stories may notice a certain tendency to rejoice in violence. For example, there is a scene at the end of *La Mort dans l'âme* (*Iron in the Soul*), when the philosophy teacher who has joined the army, attaches himself to a glamorous unit of Chausseurs and dies a Hollywood-style Hero's death shooting German soldiers one by one from a church tower: "He fired. He was cleansed. He was all-powerful. He was free". There are other writings which dwell on the details of torture. And in his *Critique*, Sartre claims that all political societies are based on terror as well as a pledge.

Sartre is far from being a pacifist. Indeed he once wrote a leading article in *Les Temps Modernes* in which he urged the Russians to take on the Americans in Vietnam, even at the risk of a third world war. The article, which appeared in August 1966, was called "*Capitulation ou contre-escalade*" and its argument was that the only effective reply to American escalation in Vietnam was counter-escalation. Sartre pointed out that there were US bases throughout the Far East, and that the Soviet artillery "already knows how to fire on a target six thousand miles away". Sartre called on the Soviets "to proclaim that there is a limit beyond which blow will be met by blow; to rely, in doing this, on the support of all those people who are sickened by the American killings no less than by their own impotence to help a Vietnam which fights for them all". He added: "Deliberately to run the risk of war today: such is the surest way of having to choose tomorrow between the reality of an imposed war or the destruction one by one of all the revolutionary states and movements of Asia".

At about the time he was writing this Sartre accepted Bertrand Russell's invitation to preside over the "War Crimes Tribunal" that Russell had set up in Sweden to investigate alleged American atrocities in Vietnam. This was a controversial enterprise. Most pacifists who opposed the war in Vietnam, and most leftists, who wanted the Viet Cong to win, were reluctant to concentrate attention on "war crimes" for the simple reason that they considered the whole American participation in the war to be crime, and they did not wish to see guilt transferred from the government in Washington to soldiers in the field. Correspondingly, people who favoured American intervention, or who were neutral in their sympathies, were unwilling to listen to atrocity stories that savoured of Communist propaganda. For these and other reasons, Bertrand Russell received less popular support than he expected for his tribunal. Sartre's collaboration is in several ways puzzling. Russell, as a pacifist and a liberal, could appeal to natural law and human rights as the basis of his indictment of "war crimes". But Sartre, the revolutionary existentialist, has always repudiated the liberal concepts of natural law and rights, which he regards as part of the ideology of the middle class—useful enough in the eighteenth century, but now completely outmoded. How could Sartre use Russell's language?

Sartre was entirely frank about his reasons for invoking liberal concepts at the "War Crimes Tribunal". His reasons were tactical. In an interview with *Le Nouvel Observateur* (November 30, 1966) he said: "We have been accused of *petit bourgeois* legalism. It is true and I accept this criticism. But who do we want to convince? . . . It is the *petit-bourgeois* masses who must be awakened and shaken up today, because their alliance—even on the home front—with the working class is so much desired. And it is by legalism that one can open their eyes".

In the event Sartre found at this period that he was losing something of his old influence over progressive middle-class opinions in France. In fact, he had never been much attuned to the sentiments of the moderate left. One example of this is the question of Israel and the Arab world. In the early 1950s, progressive French opinion was overwhelmingly pro-Israel. In the 1960s, it became fashionable to support the Arabs. By the 1970s, the Palestine guerillas had become the heroes of the moderate left, and Israel was condemned as imperialist aggressive state. Sartre, however, preserved his independent view.

Just after the war he published a remarkable essay called *Réflexions sur la question juive* in which he analysed the "Jewish question" in the light of existentialist theory. Progressive opinion at the time was apt to say that there was no such question as the Jewish question; that the Jews were just like everybody else, and the Jew should be accepted "as a man". Sartre argued instead for the recognition of the Jew "as a Jew". And Sartre has never faltered in his sympathy for Israel.

In his *Réflexions* Sartre develops the existentialist idea that a person is defined by "the gaze of the other" into the suggestion that the Jew is defined by the anti-semite. Hence to understand the "Jewish question" one must understand the anti-semite. And Sartre goes on to suggest that the French anti-semite can be recognised in sociological terms. The anti-semite belongs to the poor and of the middle-classes; he is a man who believes in bourgeois values and the right to property; but who does not have more than a trifling amount of property; his poverty is an embarrassment to him: he will not face the truth about himself—that he is a failure by the standards of the bourgeois system, nor will he agree that the system itself is wrong. So he escapes from reason altogether into the realm of passion. He seeks refuge in indignation. He hates the Jews. The miserable *petit-bourgeois* anti-semite of France makes the Jew the scapegoat for his own mediocrity just as the "White trash" of the Southern States make the Negro the scapegoat. In a sense, the anti-semite invents the Jew, because in choosing emotion rather than reason he needs someone to hate and fear.

Sartre suggests that this situation offers the Jew the existential choice of affirming or denying his Jewishness. The "authentic Jew" is he who affirms his Jewishness: the "inauthentic" Jew is the one who tries to lose his identity in some myth of universal humanity. This argument leads Sartre to give special praise to the Zionist Jew, who, in a phrase Sartre used in *Being and Nothingness*, "resolutely takes on the nature of being a Jew". After the establishment of the State of Israel, Sartre retained his admiration for the "authentic Jew", but became more critical of Zionism, especially of Zionist "chauvinism" and the Zionist policy of attracting more and more Jews from foreign countries to settle in Israel. In 1969, in the course of an interview with the Italian magazine *Quaderni del*

*Medio Oriente*\*, Sartre even went so far as to say "For me, Zionism is dead". In explaining this remark, Sartre said he agreed that Zionism had been "an advanced conception" when the great powers were colonialist. For Zionism had emerged at a time when "it was considered natural to take a piece of territory and establish oneself in some large underdeveloped country". But since then there had been the "awakening of Arab consciousness". This had the effect of making Zionism reactionary. Sartre thought it natural and reasonable that the Arabs should fear Zionism, because the Zionist aim of bringing more Jews into Israel must necessarily lead to territorial expansion at the expense of the Arabs. Sartre was ready to recognise Israel's right to accept all the Jews who might want to immigrate, but he thought it wrong that Israel should make militant Zionist politics abroad, and recruit new immigrants.

"The need for Zionism", Sartre added, "has already passed, for so long as there is no crisis of anti-semitism, and I don't think there will be any . . . the Jews of the Diaspora will prefer to stay where they are". Sartre did not think that people had been cured of

* Translated and published in English in *Midstream*, New York, August–September, 1969.

their anti-semitism, but he was confident that the kind of violent anti-semitism which would make the situation of the Jews intolerable "cannot exist in the forseeable future".

Sartre proclaimed himself less optimistic, however, about the prospects of peace in the Middle East. While he rejects the fashionable left-wing image of the Israelis as "imperialists" fighting "anti-imperialist" Arabs, he is disturbed by the economic structure of Israel, both by its dependence on the donations of American Jews, and by its pattern of trading mainly with distant industrialized countries instead of being, as he thinks it should be, part of the Middle East economy. Sartre also thinks that Israel has become less socialist since its foundation, while the Arab states have tended to become more socialist.

"I understand Israel today very well," Sartre said in his 1969 interview with the *Quaderni*. "I can equally understand how the Arabs, who have been humiliated many times by Israel's victories . . . have confounded imperialism with the presence of Israel. We are now in a period of passion on both sides, and I deplore it deeply . . . An enormous amount of time is needed to achieve something, to change mentalities".

Sartre pleading for peace in the Near East is closer to our traditional idea of a philosopher than Sartre pleading for counter-escalation in Vietnam, or Sartre exalting violence in the struggle against imperialism. Perhaps this is because our traditional idea is based on the model of Socrates; and Socrates, in his politics, we must remember, was a profound conservative. But Sartre, as we have seen, is a thoroughgoing revolutionary. In 1968, when the French workers came out in a general Strike in solidarity with the student protest movement against police repression, Sartre saw the opportunity for a revolution. The opportunity was lost, he thinks, because the Communists did not want a revolution.

This was the moment of Sartre's final break with the Communists. For years he had been trying to collaborate with them, and finding excuses for them; now he could only castigate them. What the French C.P. had done was simply to exploit the alarm the strike had caused the *bourgeoisie* to squeeze from the employers better wages and conditions of employment. The French C.P. had acted like trade unionists and reformists instead of revolutionaries, and in the process they had patched up the French capitalist system for the benefit of the *bourgeoisie* and the

Gaullist government. They had betrayed their Marxist principles.

In a pamphlet entitled *Les Communists ont peur de
la révolution*, which came out soon after the "events"
of May 1968, Sartre predicted both that the present
leadership of the left would be done for in ten years
time and that a revolutionary movement would de-
velop outside the Party. Some months later Sartre
himself took over the editorship of one such ultra-left
paper when the editors were jailed for fomenting
insurrectionary violence. Disillusioned with the Communist Party, Sartre regained after 1968 some of his
old confidence in the French working class. The
belief of Herbert Marcuse—which was also that of
Frantz Fanon—regarding the total *embourgeoise-
ment* of the Western European working class seemed
to Sartre to have been refuted by the general strike
of May 1968. He was not tempted to repeat in 1968
what he had written in 1961 about Europe being
doomed. The French working class had shown by its
general strike in May that it was capable of vigorous
"class-conscious" action. He did not lose his confidence in the new proletariat of the Third World, but
he felt more faith in the old proletariat of Europe.

Even though the Communist Party had cheated them, the French workers had vindicated their right to be considered a revolutionary class: "the wall between the workers and the intellectuals hasn't fallen", Sartre said in 1968, "but the proof has been given that it can be made to disappear in a common action".

At the end of the 1960s Sartre was more of an optimist than he was at the beginning. But the style of his politics remains distinctly apocalyptic. We may even detect a certain analogy between Sartre and the religious reformers of the sixteenth century. They wanted to restore to Christianity, grown worldly and languid, its primitive zeal for personal salvation. Sartre believes, in much the same way, that European socialism has lost its purity and sense of purpose. He does not shrink from what Camus called "fanaticism". On the contrary, Sartre believes that such a fervour is what is most needed in the world today.

# BIBLIOGRAPHY

CAMUS, ALBERT, *The Rebel* (New York: Random House, 1954).

FANON, FRANTZ, *The Wretched of the Earth*, with a preface by J.-P. Sartre. (New York: Grove Press, 1968).

SARTRE, JEAN-PAUL, *Baudelaire* (New York: New Directions, 1950).

———. *Being and Nothingness* (New York: Citadel Press, 1965).

————. *Les Communists ont peur de la révolution* (Paris, Editions Didier, 1968).

————. *The Condemned of Altona* (New York: Knopf, 1960).

————. *Cuba* (New York: Ballantine Books, 1961).

————. *The Devil and the Good Lord* and *Two Other Plays* (New York: Knopf, 1960).

————. *Essays in Aesthetics* (New York: Citadel Press, 1963).

————. *In the Mesh* (*L'Engrenage*) (London: Dakers, 1954).

————. *Kean,* or *Disorder and Genius* (London: Hamish Hamilton, 1954).

————. *Nausea* (New York: New Directions, 1949).

————. *No Exit* (*Huis-Clos*) and *Three Other Plays* (*Flies, The Dirty Hands, The Respectful Prostitute*) (New York: Random House, 1960).

————. *Paths to Freedom:*

1. *The Age of Reason* (New York: Knopf, 1947).

2. *Reprieve* (New York: Bantam, 1968).

3. *Troubled Sleep* (New York: Bantam, 1968).

————. *Saint Genet: Actor and Martyr* (New York: Braziller, 1963).

————. *Search for a Method,* Translation of the first

chapter of *Critique de la Raison Dialectique* (New York: Knopf, 1963).

———. *Situations* (New York: Braziller, 1965).

———. *What Is Literature?* (New York: Harper & Row, 1965).

———. *Words* (New York: Braziller, 1964).

71 72 73 74   12 11 10 9 8 7 6 5 4 3 2 1